Cajun Night Before Christmas ®

Cajun Night Before Christmas

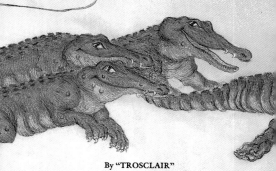

By "TROSCLAIR"

Edited by HOWARD JACOBS

Illustrated by JAMES RICE

PELICAN PUBLISHING COMPANY

Gretna 2007

First printing: October 1973
Second printing: December 1973
Third printing: June 1974
Fourth printing: August 1975
Fifth printing: August 1976
Sixth printing: September 1978
Seventh printing: September 1980
Eighth printing: October 1981
Ninth printing: October1983
Tenth printing: April 1985
Eleventh printing: September 1986
Twelfth printing: July 1988
Thirteenth printing: October 1989
Fourteenth printing: November 1990
First full-color edition: September 1992
Sixteenth printing: October 1993
Seventeenth printing: October 1995
Eighteenth printing: November 1996
Nineteenth printing: September 1998
First Christmas ornament edition: October 2000
Twentieth printing: August 2001
Second ornament printing: September 2003
Twenty-first printing: September 2004
Twenty-second printing: November 2005
Twenty-third printing: August 2007
Third ornament printing: August 2007

ISBN: 978-1-56554-849-7

Printed in Malaysia
Published by Pelican Publishing Company, Inc.
1000 Burmaster Street, Gretna, Louisiana 70053

'Twas the night before Christmas

An' all t'ru de house
Dey don't a t'ing pass
Not even a mouse.

De chirren been nezzle
Good snug on de flo'
An' Mama pass de pepper
T'ru de crack on de do'.

Den Mama in de fireplace
Done roas' up de ham
Stir up de gumbo
An' make bake de yam.

Den out on de by-you
Dey got such a clatter
Make soun' like old Boudreau
Done fall off his ladder.

I run like a rabbit
To got to de do'
Trip over de dorg
An' fall on de flo'!

As I look out de do'
In de light o' de moon
I t'ink "Manh, you crazy
Or got ol' too soon."

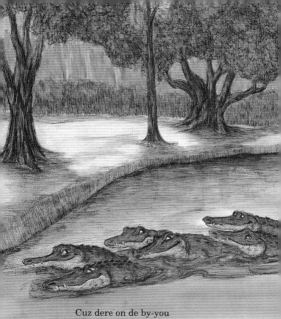

Cuz dere on de by-you
W'en I stretch ma' neck stiff
Dere's eight alligator
A pullin' de skiff.

An' a little fat drover
Wit' a long pole-ing stick
I know r'at away
Got to be ole St. Nick.

Mo' fas'er an' fas'er
De 'gator dey came
He whistle an' holler
An' call dem by name:

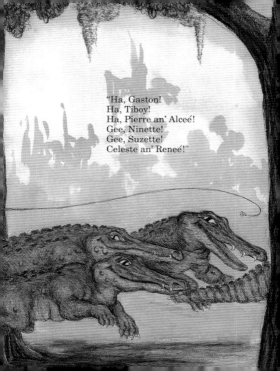

"Ha, Gaston!
Ha, Tiboy!
Ha, Pierre an' Alceé!
Gee, Ninette!
Gee, Suzette!
Celeste an' Reneé!"

"To de top o' de porch
To de top o' de wall
Make crawl, alligator,
An' be sho' you don' fall."

Like Tante Flo's cat
T'ru de treetop he fly
W'en de big ole houn' dorg
Come a run hisse'f by

Like dat up de porch
Dem ole 'gator clim!
Wit' de skiff full o' toy
An' St. Nicklus behin'.

Den on top de porch roof
It soun' like de hail
W'en all dem big 'gator
Done sot down dey tail.

Den down de chimney
I yell wit' a bam
An' St. Nicklus fall
An' sit on de yam.

"Sacre!" he axclaim
"Ma pant got a hole
I done sot ma'se'f
On dem red hot coal."

He got on his foots
An' jump like a cat
Out to de flo'
Where he lan' wit' a SPLAT!

He was dress in musk-rat
From his head to his foot
An' his clothes is all dirty
Wit' ashes an' soot.
A sack full o' playt'ing
He t'row on his back
He looked like a burglar
An' dass fo' a fack.

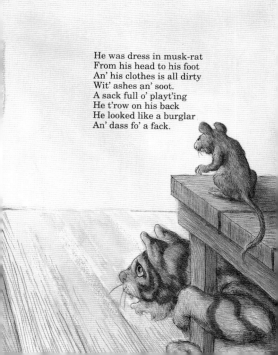

His eyes how dey shine
His dimple, how merry!
Maybe he been drink
De wine from blackberry.
His cheek was like rose
His nose like a cherry
On secon' t'ought maybe
He lap up de sherry.

Wit' snow-white chin whisker
An' quiverin' belly
He shook w'en he laugh
Like de stromberry jelly!
But a wink in his eye
An' a shook o' his head
Make my confi-dence dat
I don' got to be scared.

He don' do no talkin'
Gone straight to his work
Put playt'ing in sock
An' den turn wit' a jerk.

He put bot' his han'
Dere on top o' his head
Cas' an eye on de chimney
An' den he done said:
"Wit' all o' dat fire
An' dem burnin' hot flame
Me I ain' goin' back
By de way dat I came."

So he run out de do'
An' he clim' to de roof
He ain' no fool, him
For to make one more goof.

He jump in his skiff
An' crack his big whip.
De 'gator move down
An' don' make one slip.

An' I hear him shout loud
As a splashin' he go

"Merry Christmas to all
'Til I saw you some mo'!"